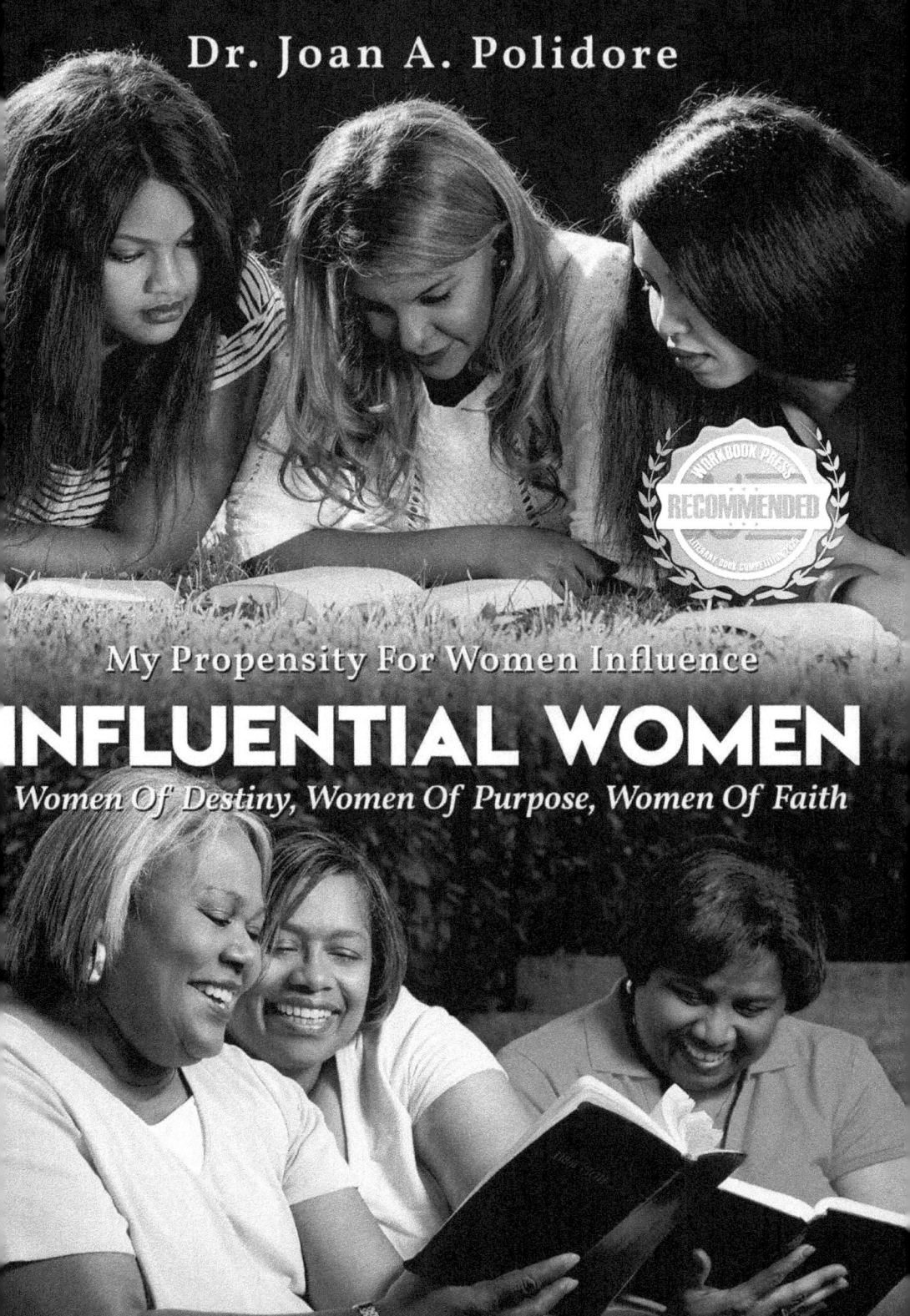

Dr. Joan A. Polidore

My Propensity For Women Influence

INFLUENTIAL WOMEN

Women Of Destiny, Women Of Purpose, Women Of Faith

WORKBOOK PRESS
RECOMMENDED

WORKBOOK PRESS LLC
187 E Warm Springs Rd,
Suite B285 Las Vegas NV 89119 USA

Website: https://workbookpress.com/
Hotline: 1-888-818-4856
Email: admin@workbookpress.com

Ordering Information:

Quantity sales. Special discounts are available on quantity purchases by corporations, associations, and others. For details, contact the publisher at the address above.

Library of Congress Control Number:

ISBN-13:   978-1-965732-32-8   Paperback Version

REV. DATE: 02/21/2025

Dr. Joan A. Polidore

My Propensity For Women Influence

INFLUENTIAL WOMEN

Women Of Destiny, Women Of Purpose, Women Of Faith

CONTENTS

BIOGRAPHY

DR. JOAN A. POLIDORE is the daughter of Mr. Cyril and Christiana Dejean. She is the ninth of sixteen children. She was born at Morne Prosper on the Caribbean Island of Dominica. The village was called Morne Prosper because it was a prolific village. Her parents were devoted Roman Catholics and so she was not allowed to read the bible. However, Dr. Polidore was determined to study the "Word of God".

In 1979 Dr. Polidore relocated to the USA due to the destruction of Dominica by Hurricane David. Dr. Polidore is married to Pastor Julian Polidore and are the elated parents of four professional daughters, Beverly, Julia, Amanda, and Deborah.

Dr. Polidore started her teaching career after graduating from High school, then taught as a public school teacher at Morne Prosper in 1964 and Hostel pre-school from 1970 to 1979. After moving to the USA, she attended Empire State College where she studied nursing and worked at A Holly Patterson Geriatric Center in 1983. She also worked as a Family Care Provider supervising mentally challenged clients for twenty-five years.

Dr. Polidore was a member of the Gospel Light House Assembly and was a committed servant for the Lord. While there, she attended Bethel Bible Institute and acquired her Associate Degree in Theology; in 1999.

Dr. Polidore was a member of the Abundant Life Ministry and served as Evangelist and Dean of the Bible School.

In 2000, she acquired her Bachelor's Degree in Theology at Vision International. She was ordained Chaplain by the Christian Chaplain Association of New York. Dr. Polidore was an ordained Elder and together with her husband founded Agape Ministries Inc. and Christian Academy where she served as Pastor, Youth Advocate, and the school Administrator.

Under the leadership of Dr. Polidore and her husband, the ministry gave birth to a Youth Center, Soup kitchen, and Homeless Shelter. In 2013, Dr. Polidore acquired her Masters of Divinity at Southwest Bible College and Seminary.

In 2014, Dr. Polidore returned to her native island of Dominica where she and her husband are presently pastoring the Warner Pentecostal Church. In 2015, Dr. Polidore acquired her Doctorate Degree in Christian Counseling and has already conducted many sessions in counseling in the U S A and Dominica. Dr. Polidore is the author of the Book " The Ministry of Hospitality" and anticipating the publication of "Influential Women, Women of Purpose, Women of Faith."

INTRODUCTION

BIBLE WOMEN FOR THE MOST part appeared to have been subordinate figures to men, particularly in the Old Testament, although there were women like Miriam, Esther, and Deborah in the Old Testament, and Priscilla and Lydia in the New Testament who were not subordinated.

According to Edith Deen, in her book, "All the Women of the Bible", in the ancient Near East, up until about 3,500 years ago, women had no property rights. If a man died leaving no sons, his daughters did not inherit what he had left. The first women, to declare their rights on the death of their father were the five daughters of Zelophehad; Mahlah, Noah, Hoglah, Milcah, and Tirzah.

Their father, a Manassite, had died in the wilderness and the daughters explained that he was not in the company of Koran, who had rebelled against Moses. Because their father had not died therefore for any cause that doomed their family or their inheritance, they declared they were entitled to what he had left. They were numbered among all those in the tribe who either were twenty or would be twenty by the time the land was distributed.

They knew that existing customs would have no property rights in the new land, but they took courage and marched before Moses, the priest Eleazer, and the congregation and stated, their case publicly. Numbers 27:4 states, "Give unto us, therefore, a possession among the brethren of our father. Why should the name of our father be done away from among his family, because he had no sons declaring their rights?" It has been proven that these women were effective leaders.

The writer's conclusion is that these five daughters were unique among the Bible women who stood for their rights because their father did not die off in the rebellion life of the company of Moses. It took great courage to begin anything. Since it was customary that women could not have property rights; murmuring, complaining among them could not do it. They gathered sufficient strength, went to Moses and the priest Eleazer, and made their first request known which a possession, among the brethren was. Leaders do make things happen. By going to Moses a wise man of God, he took the matter to the Omniscient God who revealed to Moses that it was right for the five daughters to have their possession. Mahal, Noah, Hoglah, Milcah, and Tirzah were the first women to declare their rights and by doing so, their father's name was maintained in the family. In addition, other women could be motivated by the power of their influence and become great leaders in the ministry.

According to Webster's Dictionary, the word "equal" means, of the same measurement, quantity, or values another, having the same privileges or rights". The word "equal" has often been misunderstood and referred to as the helper. "In Women Mentoring Women" by Vickie Kraft, she felt that the woman was created to be a helper suitable to Adam and not an inferior person. The writer's definition of equal is helping out, giving advice, not taking over, being a part of, and sharing with the one being helped. One of the benefits of great women leaders conferred in the ministry today is that women live according to their zealous persistence and aim for their sense of things.

The writer's view is that the first woman, "Eve", was the cause of the subordination of men when she desired to withdraw from the protection of her husband and rebelled against God's command. As a result of Eve's disobedience, this is what God pronounced on the woman (Genesis 3:16), "Unto the woman he said, "I will greatly multiply their sorrow and their conception; in sorrow, thou shalt bring forth children; and thy desire shall be to thy husband, and he shall rule over thee". This was God's command for the woman to be submissive to her husband (Ephesians 5:22). But men generally have taken it a little too far and have abused the mandate.

He continued to say, they were among the most conspicuous example of transforming power and influence of Christianity. The pagan Librans's exclaimed, "What power women these Christians have"

According to the Bible, and modern-day history, there is proof that women can be effective leaders equal to men, both in the secular and spiritual realm. History has provided a great number of women in leadership and positions, and their accomplishments have spoken for them. God in His Majestic Omniscience has chosen to qualify women to work alongside men to carry out His plan and purpose for His glory. Since God is no respecter of persons (Roman 2:11) and therefore makes no distinction. It can be seen that women are effective leaders equal to men in the ministry.

PREFACE

THIS BOOK IS ABOUT THE POWER OF WOMEN INFLUENCE AND HOW THEIR INFLUENCE HAS THE POTENTIAL TO HELP PEOPLE DISCOVER THEIR POTENTIAL AND FIND THEIR DESTINY IN CHRIST JESUS.

THE INFLUENTIAL WoMAN, THE WoMAN of Faith, The Woman of Destiny. This book has the potential to change lives and help women reach their destiny due to its basis on sound biblical principles, and shows the secularist how women can use their influence in whatever way big or small to create change.

I was attending Long Beach High in New York, when an assignment was given to me. I was told to write a letter to my Mayor indicating my interest in something I would like to see in my community. I petitioned Alberny for schools to wear uniforms. Read the details in chapter 3 This Book Is About the Power of Women Influence and How Their Influence Has the Potential To Help People Discover Their Potential And Find Their Destiny In Christ Jesus.

Chapter 1

EXPERIENCING THE POWER OF WOMEN INFLUENCE

'IN THE BEGINNING, GOD CREATE the heaven and the earth"(Gen. 1:1). However, someone had to exercise the power given by God and take dominion over what He had created. Then God said "Let us make man in Our image, according to our likeness; let them have dominion over the fish of the sea, over the birds of the air... So God created man in His own image; in His image created He male and female, He created them" (Gen. 1:26-27). WE ARE ALL SONS AND HEIRS OF GOD. (Gal. 3: 28)

"There is neither Jew nor Greek, there is neither slave nor free, there is neither male nor female; for we are all one in Christ Jesus. "However, God separated their purpose, for us to fulfill our purpose in life He gave the Power of Authority to the men and the Power of Influence to the women. For this cause, "God said it is not good for the man to be alone, I will make him a helper comparable to him." In virtue of the Power of Authority, the man makes the decisions and the Power of Influence helps makes and carry out the decision by the rib who was taken out of the man whom he called woman. Therefore, shall a man leave his father and his mother and shall be joined to his wife, and they shall become one flesh". (Gen.2:21-24).

GOD'S PURPOSE FOR WOMEN

God has a specific plan and a purpose for every woman created in his image. "I know the thoughts that I think towards you, says the Lord, thoughts of peace, and not of evil, to give you a future and a hope" (Jer. 29:11). Yet we still struggle to understand our true uniqueness and embrace our differences from man and our character. The woman was beguiled, and influenced her husband to disobey God's command. (THE RUIN OF MAN) "Therefore, just as through one-man sin entered the world, and death through sin, and thus death spread to all men because all have sinned" (Rom. 5:12). However, God in His mercy for His great love wherewith He loves us sent His Son to redeem those who were under the law that we might receive the adoption as sons. "But when the fullness of the time had come, God sent forth His Son born of a woman, born under the law" (Gal.4:4). The man was created before the woman. Because the man needed a companion and a helper, God caused the man to have a deep sleep. From him he created a woman, a helper comparable to him (Gen. 2:8

20), Man is incomplete without a woman. A woman's unique make-up qualifies her for special purposes in all areas of her life; e.g. motherhood, teacher, doctor, counselor, help-mate, companion, intercessor, financial manager. God said it is not good for man to be alone. The "rib" is the supportive system of the family, home, the community, and the nation.

Jesus esteemed the purpose of women and the power of their influence highly and allowed them to accompany Him and His disciples on their journeys (Luke 8:1-3). Making the best use of their influence by multiplying them.

Women who understand their purpose can function independently using their influence and power productively in every aspect of life, spiritually and socially to bring honor and glory to God. God's specific purpose for women is accomplished; (A) when a woman delights to do God's will by accepting and appreciating her power and influence and her resources as well. (B) By aligning herself with God's perspectives. Her influence will be at it's pick when she shares with her followers and allows them to collaborate in her vision. "The hand that rocks the cradle rules the World." By: Curtis Hanson.

Chapter 2

CHARACTERISTICS IN DISPLAYING INFLUENCE

- Women have a tendency to crave for materialism: Eve saw that the tree was good for food, that it was pleasant to the eyes and a tree desirable to make one wise, she took of its fruit and ate. She also gave to her husband with her and he ate (Gen.3:6).

- Women of purpose should not love the world. "Do not love the world or the things that are in the world. If anyone loves the world the love of the Father is not in him.; And the world is passing away, and the lust of it; but he who does the will of God abides forever" (1John 2: 15 - 17). Lot's wife, perished because her heart was in Sodom, where your treasure is there will your heart be also (Gen. 19:26).

Women with a carnal mentality have a tendency to come between a man and his God. David's wife despised him for dancing in worship expressing his gratitude to his God. (2Sam.6:16)." Solomon" the wisest man that ever lived, ignored the command of God because of the influence of his many ungodly wives. Many foreign women caused him to go into idolatry and rejected the Lord's counsel which brought God's judgment and chasing upon his Kingdom; wherefore the kingdom was divided. (1Kings 11: 1, 4-9). "Better to dwell in a corner of a housetop, than in a house shared with a contentious woman"(Pro.21:9). Yet if a man finds a wife, he finds a good thing and obtains favor of the Lord. (Pro.18:22).

- Mary and Martha were very intimate with Jesus that they felt comfortable in questioning His authority and by so doing they wanted to be His advisors. (John 11:38-39).

Women are very concerned to live a good impression. " For the good that I will do, I do not, but the evil I will not do, that I practice" (Rom.7:19). Women are prone to show favoritism, and do it professionally." And Isaac loved Esau because he ate of his game, but Rebekah loved Jacob and caused him to deceive his father" (Gen. 25:28).

Chapter 3

THIS BOOK IS ABOUT POTENTIAL TO CHANGE LIVES BY HELPING WOMEN DISCOVER THEIR IDENTITY AND REDIRECTING THEIR PERSPECTIVE IN LIFE

MANY WOMEN MINISTERED TO JESUS "AND certain women who had been healed of evil spirits and infirmities. Mary Magdalene, out of whom had come seven demons and Joanna the wife of Chuza, Herod's steward, and Susanna, and many others who provided for Him from their substance" (Matt. 27:55, Luke 8:1:3). Jesus approved of their influence and liberated them to use their Power and Influence in Ministry.

The author wants her influence to motivate women to use their influence in whatever way big or small. I was attending Long Beach High School New York, when an assignment was given to me, to write a letter to my Mayor indicating my interest in something I would like to see in my community.

My propensity was to see our school children wearing uniforms. I immediately took the idea to my Mayor, I hand-delivered the letter to him myself. He gave me an astonishing look and told me to take it to the Superintendent of Schools. I went the same day to the Superintendent who asked me a few questions; my answer was that it would eliminate the peer pressure among students and made it cost-effective to parents. And I am from the West Indies and we wore uniforms at school. Therefore, I was passionate about school uniforms for my children.

Besides all his questions were that, "do you know that this is a Democratic country? People are free to wear what they want. I said yes Sir but this is my passion and I am asking you to give it a thought. He handed me the letter back and told me to take it to my school Parent Teacher's Association in Roosevelt New York, where I lived at that time, and if they approve it came back to him. I was confident as I began praying for favor on my way to the school; low and behold as we know it "freedom of choice", some were for and some opposed it but I got the majority approval and I was successful. I requested an approval letter from the president and took it back to the Superintendent of Schools who in return forward my request to the Mayor and a few months later it was marked official the schools in the community of Roosevelt New York were free to wear uniform to school, that was a great incentive my victory was worn. I do want to encourage women to emulate my courage and perseverance to achieve their goals in whatever they aspire to accomplish.

HOW AGAPE MINISTRY BEGAN: VISION, PRAYER, PERSEVERANCE, COURAGE, AND FAITH IN GOD.

I HAD A VISION in 1999: That only faith in God could execute. "But also for this reason giving all diligence add to your faith virtue and virtue knowledge, to knowledge self-control, and self-control perseverance and perseverance, godliness, and to godliness brotherly kindness and brotherly kindness love. For if these things are in you and abound you shall neither be barren nor unfruitful" (2 Peter 1: 5-8).

The Vision was a mandate from the Lord; "Go to the street corners and gather the children from the streets of Roosevelt New York, to teach them the word of God. They were given a snack and assistance with their homework. MY program was structured by this system, (1) Spiritually (2) Academically, (3) Socially and Emotionally by these guide-lines students could make indicative choices to be prolific citizens and to dream, achieve, to learn, and to aspire for greatness. What a command, however by adding virtue to my faith I obeyed the Lord. And by the power of my influence, my husband united with me; and the Lord made a way, for us to purchase a building in 2001. "The Woman of Faith", "The Woman of Influence" and "The Woman of Destiny" made this happened. The Ministry expanded to "Agape Christian Academy, Youth Center, Food Pantry, Soup Kitchen, and Homeless shelter for young men who were incrassated who were most likely to be rejected by family members and their community.

Through the power of influence, women can achieve anything they desire to do with their confidence in God and abiding in his word which will make them self-sufficient, independent, prolific, and efficient women to embark on anything they desire. "The eyes of all look expectantly to you. And You give them their food in due season. You open Your hand, And satisfy the desire of every living thing" (Psalm 145:15-16).

WOMAN: MERRIAM WEBSTER'S COLLEGIATE DICTIONARY DEFINITION OF WOMAN: (1) AN ADULT FEMALE PERSON (2) WIFE, MOTHER A WOMAN BELONGING TO A PARTICULAR CATEGORY AS BY BIRTH, RESIDENCE MEMBERSHIP, OR OCCUPATION USED IN COMBINATION AS COUNCILWOMAN, WOMANKIND DISTINCTIVELY FEMININE IN NATURE.

THE BIBLES' DEFINITION OF WOMAN: A FEMALE ADULT:

However, the word woman is sometimes used in the Bible to refer to a weak and helpless man (Isa. 3:12: 19:16).

To understand the Old Testament view of women one must turn to the book of Genesis. When God created man He created both male and female (Gen. 1:27; 5:2). Both were created in God's image and were given the responsibility of exercising authority over God's creation. The man was created before the woman. Because the man needed companionship and a helper… (Gen. 2:18-20) Man is incomplete without a woman. Because she is called a helper does not imply that she is inferior to man. The same Hebrew word translated as a helper is used of God in His relationship to Israel in (Psalms 33:20; 70:5). The culture that developed around the Israelites in ancient times did not always have this perspective of a woman.

Certain Old Testament passages tend to reflect an attitude that a woman was little more than a thing and that a woman should be entirely subordinate to man. This tendency became pronounced before the coming of Christ. (It is said that a certain Jew prayer was "Thanked thee that I am not a woman"). Jesus lived and taught a better way, the way of LOVE, FORGIVENESS, HOPE, AND COMFORT. He allowed women to accompany Him and His disciples on their journeys (Luke 8:1-3). He spoke with the Samaritan woman and gave her "LIVING WATER"; without condemning her of her lifestyle. Because of his attributes, she was able to redirect her perspective and live a better life.

She did not keep this experience to herself but ran to the community and proclaimed that the Messiah had come. Jesus identified Himself as Messiah and the people believed in Him and also experienced sins forgiven and the Hope of Eternal Life. His disciples were not too happy with the fact that Jesus interacted with the woman since in that era Samaritans and Jews did not have a good relationship. However, Jesus' love transcended all cultural and religious doctrines. His mission is souls "For the Son of man is came to seek and to save that which was lost" (Luke 19:10).

Even today Jesus is still calling women who are desirous of following Him and make Him known to all who believe and accept Him as saviour. Jesus gave an example to His disciples by permitting Mary to sit at His feet identified herself as a disciple also. He encouraged Martha that she should do likewise; proving to His disciples that God makes no distinction between male or female. (Luke 10:38-42). Although the Jews segregated the women in both Temples and Synagogues the early church did not (Acts 12:1-17; 1 Cor.11:2-16). Paul wrote there is neither Jew nor Greek (Gal.3:28) The Apostle Paul spoke of their custom; they should be submissive (1 Cor. 14:34 – 35); (1Tim. 2:11:12).

In Galatians, Apostle Paul was stating the general principle that men and women are equal. Paul requested the women to be submissive to their husbands to preserve order within the church and to be a witness to outsiders. Some of the finest leaders in Israel were women, considering that the culture was male-dominated. Military victories were sometimes won because of the courage of one woman (Judges 4-5; 9:54; Esther 4:16). God revealed His word through Prophetesses (Jud 4:4; Luke 2:36; Acts 21:9). God used Priscilla and her husband to explain the way of God more accurately to Apollos the preacher (Acts 18:26). The heroes of faith mentioned in Hebrews 11 includes Sarah; Moses' mother and Rahab the harlot. Jeremiah called for the skillful and wailing women to pray during the Plight of Israel and to teach their daughters how to pray also (Jer.9:17).

Chapter 4

GOD MAKES NO DISTINCTION: OLD TESTAMENT EXAMPLES

VICKIE KRAFT, IN HER BOOK, "Women Mentoring Women," said that the Old Testament qualified women as effective leaders in the ministry upon the working of the Holy Spirit and obedience to the Lord. It is interesting to note, in (Genesis 21: 12), that God commanded Abraham to obey Sarah. Sarah's relationship with her husband is a real role model to follow concerning relationships with our husbands, (I Peter 3:1-6) Sarah's behavior reflected godly submission but did not allow her to be taken advantage of. Although Sarah was outspoken and feisty she was protective and supportive of her husband. Likewise, Women are qualified equally as leaders in ministry because in scripture God uses women in key ministry for Him. A woman is qualified and equipped to lead equally with a man by "redemption".

"In Micah 6: 4 God told Israel that he set before them Leaders as Moses, Aaron, and Miriam." In the latter passage, Miriam is called one of the leaders of Israel. Women in the Bible called "skilled" voluntarily contributed their possessions and worked with their hands in constructing the Tabernacle. (Exodus 35:21-22. 25-26). Women served in the doorway of the Tabernacle. The same word for service was used for them as for the Levites, (Exodus 38:8; I Samuel 2:22), "Hannah was a woman of total commitment to prayer and passion for God. Hannah had access to God, made a vow, and kept it. Due to her faith and commitment to God, her son Samuel become a leader in Israel who turned the nation around.

Vickie Kraft, "Women Mentoring Women". "Out of the contest and conquest came the moral purification, its present nation is an inspiring genius who was a woman. Dynamic in the leadership of her nation. No character in the Old Testament stands out bolder than Deborah, prophetess, ruler, and warrior, her song is immortal because her life was dedicated to God and her deeds heroic and sublime. Deborah stands as a true woman equal of influence with her leadership ability. God used the strong character in Deborah to deliver a real sting to the forces of evil which surrounded Israel, for the meaning of Deborah's name meant "bee".

"Shepherd's Notes", mentioned that Esther was a Jewish orphan raised by her Uncle in Persia, and later became Queen. Courageously, Esther embraced the opportunity to go from "rags to riches". Through the work of the Mighty God in her life, deliverance was brought to God's people. God used Esther because she was a woman who was willing to sacrifice her life for her people and do God's will. Throughout the book of Esther, the story recounts a courageous young woman who risked her life and comfortable position to save her people. The position was given to her by God to serve others, Esther was brought before the King because of her exceptional beauty, and her lovely form and features. Later on, it was understood that Esther was related to the Jew Mordecai, who wisely advised her to keep her Jewish identity a secret since the Jews were a minority people in Persia.

Already it was obvious that God was at work in the selection process. Esther's position as Queen could enable her to save the Jews from Haman who was the second most powerful man in the empire, however, God's power was greater. Esther obtained favor from the King, Esther's position was considered and the circumstance was quickly changed.

Esther's nationality was revealed as she pleaded for her people. Since Haman's decree was irrevocable, the King instructed Esther and Mordecai to write a counter decree which would also carry the King's name sealed with his signet ring giving favor to the Jews. Esther was determined to win the King's heart by her strength and righteous influence for the good of others, even if it meant risking her own life she was a woman of faith.

Chapter 5

THE POWER OF WOMEN INFLUENCE: MODERN DAY WOMEN IN POLITICS

THE MOST INFLUENTIAL EVENTS IN the 20th century in the history of women; noted in the Book "A Century of Women" by a spastic group who described women as those who pursued careers, sick souls suffering from lack of love who was trying to intimate men. Another group viewed women as victims of a modern industrial society that expects them to behave like feminists who wanted to compete with men in their profession. However, they were proven wrong.

However Modern women have risen to the challenge, with much courage, perseverance, and determination to change the cycle of home mom or housewives. They have ascended to the political arena. They have fought violently to breach the gap like their parents. They have attained the heights of Astronauts Sally Ride first in astronaut in 1980. Women founded the Women's Political Campaigns 1980, they founded the Women's Political Campaigns 1980-1989 (Emily). The Daytona Normal and Industrial Institute for negro Girls was found during the 1900-1909 by Mary McLeod Bethune. The first Study of Occupational disease was founded by Dr. Alice Hamilton. Betty Crocker, advertised symbol off Domesticity, 1920-1929 made her first appearance to name a few.

The Power of women's influence has reformed womanhood and society in its entirety, through privileges, rights, and indicative choices. They have led the way for the right to vote, sexual freedom, job opportunities, and security provided by laws that abolished discrimination and sexual harassment on the job. Women have educated themselves and were daring for what they wanted, making history to "A Women's World Today".

According to Deborah G. Felder; Ann May Jarvis (1864-1948) was given the honor of being credited with the courage and the persistence to accomplish A Day when mothers would be treasured with gratitude and appreciation.

Ann Mary Jarvis nursed her mother until death. But she thought she could have done more for her. Therefore, at her mother's memorial service, she gave white carnations to all the mothers which were her mother's favorite flower which symbolized Mother's Day -The white carnation also typified "THE BEAUTY, TRUTH, AND FIDELITY OF MOTHER'S LOVE".

However, many before her made the suggestion and strive for the Day but were not successful. They were women like Mary T. Sasseen of Kentucky who on her mother's birthday gathered some teachers to celebrate, in honor of Mother's Day but her idea was not well accepted. Robert Cummins, about two years later Universalist Baltimore Sunday school made the same suggestion to observe a National Day for mothers; the suggestion did not create much excitement at that time.

Nine women, who changed modern America by Karenna Gore Schiff, are noted in her book "Lighting the Way." Ida B. Well was a young school teacher who rode the train with a first-class ticket from Memphis to Tennessee but one-day history was formed; she was dragged from the train because she was not permitted to ride as first class.

However, she would not take it lightly as she was humiliated by being desecrating. She filed a lawsuit against the Chesapeake Railroad and although she was awarded, that behavior continued on numerous accessions living Ida as a victim.

Being victimized, discourage, and perplex, she turned her deli more to wisdom and bravery; challenging discrimination daring to stand alone. She made her way to her propensity, discovering more and more of the horrific torture, murder, and inhuman treatment blacks went through. During the ten years of the Chesapeake Railroad incident. Well became violent and forcefully in her adventure; naming her the leading and lynching activist, and courageous controversial distinguished not only in the United State but also in the United Kingdom.

With perseverance, Ida B. Well was able to counter the lies told by many in the mainstream press and embark on a career that sprung myriad of years later. She made countless speeches, published articles, and assays organized a network of clubs and community organizations for African-Americans. She kept on aiming for higher heights and worked with prominent activities such as Susan B. Anthony, Frederick Douglass, and W.E. Du Bois, in that era. However, working with that class she dared to be her Person, Writing, Speaking, or Organizing, she faced many challenges, oppositions but dare to make the sky her limitation.

According to Karenna Gore Schiff in her book "Lighting the Way" 1888 Well was contributing to black newspapers around the country, including the Indianapolis World, the Chicago Conservator, the A. M-E. Church Review, the Detroit Plain Dealer, and the People's Choice, often writing under the pen name "Iola". She attended the National Colored Press Association meeting and networking with editors and journalists from all over the country.

Well's hard work and courageous outlook in life caused her to triumphant over the obstacles and bridging the generation gap brought her to the point where she widely cited and often praised, earning the respect of her mostly male colleagues. It was said that a correspondent for the New Orleans Weekly Pelican proclaimed in 1887 that the daring and importunate Ida Well was the most prominent correspondent at present connected with the Negro press.

T. Thomas Fortune editor of the New York Age highly commented on her achievement by stated that "Iola trap" became famous as one of the few of our women who handled a goose quill with a diamond point as handily as any man in newspaper work. She has plenty of nerve and is as sharp as a steel trap. It was said of another writer, she was "The Princess of the Press" and an inspiration to the younger writers.

The years of dolls, sub-servants, and peering alongside the Mayflower came to an end; by some courageous, heartbreaking, and daring women who made history in the lives of woman's world in America.

According to Gail Collins in her book "America's Women." It is said that Gail Collins, an editorial at the New York Times, charts a journey that shows how women lived, what they cared about, what they wanted to change, and how women lived what they cared about, and how they felt about marriage, sex and work.

She painted a beautiful picture going way back to the "Lost Colony of Roanoke" and the early Southern "Tobacco Bridges". Pointing out all the different reasons and circumstances what women needed to change. Therefore, she fought aggressively for a reformation in their condition during that era.

In the 70s America's Women were identified by the way they lived, by the dress they wore, fashion design, medical advances, rules of hygiene, social theories about sex, and courtship. However, Collins dared to change that because women are not what they wear but who they are. They are women of influence, because of the role they played; they are the pillars of society, the community, the home, in the church, and even at the workplace.

God the surgeon general of all surgeon generals, the first to perform surgery in the Garden of Eden took a rib from Adam the very first man He created, and formed a woman. The strength of the man is in a physical form, therefore he needed the woman to complete him. (Gen. 2:22). That "Rib" represents strength, courage, wisdom, endurance, perseverance, warriors, wailing, mourning, skillful, these are some of the characteristics that make women stand as pillars of strength today.

Just as the rib is the supportive system of the body so women are empowered to demonstrate their strength which is the basis for creating change for using their influence to create change making history in the "Woman's World Today."

The first woman astronaut, Sally Ride was born in Encino California in 1951; her dream was to be an astronaut from a child. It is stated in the book "A Century of Women" by Deborah G. Field that Sally Ride was an exceptional student and athlete, a star college tennis player, and a member of the Stanford University women's rugby team. She graduated from Stanford in 1973, earning a BS in physics and a BA in English literature. She remained at Stanford to gain her Ph.D. in astrophysics as she was working there as an assistant teacher and researcher when she was selected as an astronaut.

After she was named as the first American woman scheduled to fly in the space shuttle, media attention leading up to her flight was intense. With perseverance at age thirty-one, Ride was the youngest American to go into orbit. She also took part in the development of two communications satellites and the deployment and retrieval of the German-built shuttle Pallet Satellite.

The challenges she faced molted her character to aim for higher heights, braving the storms of her achievement; lead Kathryn Sullivan who was her class member to emulate her and become the first American woman to walk in space.

"The vocation of American women has been pretentiously changed the course in an economic depression, war, social imperatives, and technological advance. By women who endeavored to collaborate in groups such as the "Women Trade Union League". The National Organization for Women to reform the quality of life and empower women for freedom to embark on any field or career they so desire to pursuit.

Chapter 6

WOMEN IN POLITICS

WOMEN OBTAINED FAVOR WITH GOD through prayer, the travailing woman; worn a triumphant victory. And Hannah prayed and said "My heart rejoiceth in the LORD, mine horn is exalted in the LORD; my mouth is enlarged over my enemies because I rejoice in thy salvation. There is none holy like the LORD; for there is none beside thee, neither is there any rock like our God. Talk no more so exceeding proudly; let not arrogance come out of your mouth; for the LORD is a God of knowledge, and by Him, actions are weighted. The bows of the mighty men are broken, and they that stumbled are girded with strength."

"They who were full have hired out themselves for bread, and they who were hungry ceased to hunger; so that the barren hath borne seven; and she who hath many children languished. The LORD maketh poor, and maketh rich; He bringeth low and lifteth up. He raiseth up the poor out of the dust, and lifteth up the beggar from the refuse, to set them among princes, and to make them inherit the throne of glory; for The Pillars of the Earth are the LORD'S and he hath set the world upon them" (1Sam. 2: I-8).

Women have risen from being servants, housewives from the "Lost Colony of Roanoke" and the early "South Tobacco Planters" and the cotton picking to Women in the White House, State women, vice president, governors, senators, judges, and Council women.

This is a word of wisdom to all young women; please do not terminate your child because that child that was murdered might be the next senator or the next president of the United State. It is said that "The Hands that rock the cradle rule the world." Jochebed, Moses' mother was a woman of faith, a woman of observation, a woman of great courage, and perseverance who defied the king's command to save her son's life for she noticed that he was a proper child with leadership ability. So she hid her son in the house for three months and when he could no longer stay in the house she made him a basket and put him on the Nile River in the care of his sister. When this man "Moses" grew up he was instrumental (in the hands of God) to be the great leader, prophet, and priest of the nation Israel and delivered them from the bondage of slavery from the hand of Pharaoh in Egypt (Ex. 2:1- 10).

Mr. John and his wife Angelina Rice did not anticipate that their baby girl would grow up to be that powerful and prestigious in U.S. politics. "Train up a child in the way he should go, and when he is old he will not depart from it" (Pro. 22:6). John and his wife were very supportive of their daughter Condoleezza at an early age. Whatever she was interested in they were there to sear and guide her through it. In the heat of prejudice and racism, her parents did their very best to shield her from the abuse that African-Americans were experiencing. They fought violently, to be victors and not victims despite their challenges. Condoleezza's parents were both college graduates and motivated their daughter to pursue higher education; they often told her of the family history. Therefore, she emulated her parents and excelled even in elementary school in academics.

It is stated by Christin Ditchfield that Condoleezza Rice faced many challenges and rascal barriers in high school but none of those things moved her. Moreover, she was successful in achieving a college career. With perseverance, Condoleezza triumphant overall odds and became an international figure in political affairs. Rice was instrumental in advising President George H.W. Bush during his summit meetings with Soviet President Mikhail Gorbachev. She had many views in common with President W. Bush on issues including a foreign policy which he acknowledged as an asset to his ministry as President. Condoleezza Rice was President Bush's great moral supporter; "The Power of women influence*' Rice's encouraged him to be hopeful when he was in despair on foreign relations issues while he was on the campaign trail. Her knowledge and expertise open many doors for her to serve in political affairs. The governor of California appointed her to a committee focused on political reform. Rice speech was profound and persuasive at the Republican National Convention in 200 which brought her respect, and honored her achievement as a black minority woman.

God honors those who honor Him. Mr. and Mrs. John Rice obeyed God in training their daughter in the fair and admonishment of the LORD. "Train up a child in the way he should go and when he is old, he will not depart from it" (Pro. 22:6). Therefore, God gave him the privilege before his death to see his daughter became a very powerful figure in Washington D.C. and glorifying God who gave her the ability to accomplish her goal.

Because God gives wisdom and out our His mouth comes knowledge and understand. "A man's gift makes room for him and bringeth him before great men" (Pro. 18:16). Condoleezza Rice was appointed as the nation's first female national security advisor by President George W. Bush. Rice honored God who blessed her with her gift and exercised the power of her influence in the State Capital. "Every good and perfect gift is from above. and cometh down from the Father of lights, with whom is no variableness, neither shadow of turning" (James1:17). A gift is not being hidden but to be used accordingly.

In the parable of the talent, the man who had received the one talent did not use it but hidden it which was not pleasing to his master, because there he did not make any profit for his master. However, the one who was given five used them to the best of his ability and was successful in gaining another five talents which were pleasing to his master. For the LORD delights in the prosperity of his people. "And so the one that had received five talents came and brought other five talents, saying LORD, thou delivered unto me five talents; behold I have gained beside them five talents more. His Lord said unto him, well done, thou good and faithful servant; thou has been faithful over a few things. I will make you the ruler over many things. Enter into the joy of thy Lord." (Matt. 25:23).

It has been stated that we must actively recruit more women to run for Political Office in virtue of the fact that women are built to be the supportive system of society. In families where both adults are working, generally in high-level careers, women are 12 times more likely than men to be responsible for the majority of household tasks, and more than 10 times more likely to be responsible for the majority of child care responsibilities.

As a businesswoman from Chicago says: "Women are responsible not only for the family but also for earning half the money."

There are yet several single women who does an enormous job raising their children and being prolific community members. They are courageous, persevering, and brilliant, knowing how to travail in adversity. They are influential in making followers. The number in congress has tripled over the past 20 twenty years. According to the Library of Congress, the Democratic congressional delegation, which is the largest state party delegation in Congress is comprised of more women than men. From the time World Ward II folded the number of women serving in the U.S. House of Representatives and Senate has increased to more than 80 percent. An effort to increase federal funding for programs to research AIDS and provide services for those suffering from the disease.

In 1998 Pelosi a kind and compassionate woman, as a member of the House Intelligence Committee, traveled to Guatemala to investigate the assassination of an activist Roman Catholic bishop, Juan Gerardo Conedera.

There is a picture of a woman of influence who was faced with the odds of a wife, mother, and a legal staffer for the House Judiciary Committee.

According to Joyce Milton in her investigation of Hillary Rodham Clinton in her book. "The First Partner". In 1998, Hillary Rodham Clinton became the most admired woman in America while also becoming the most visibly wronged wife in the world. Sanding by her husband, President Bill Clinton, as she and the nation learned the truth behind the Monica Lewinsky scandal. The First lady was both a dutiful spouse and a passionate defense attorney, two roles she had played on numerous occasions during this tumultuous yet politically unified relationship.

"For if you forgive men their trespasses, your heavenly Father will also forgive you; But if you forgive not men their trespasses, neither will your Father forgive your trespasses." (Matt. 6: 14-15)."

Hillary Rodham Clinton did what the Word of God sated to do because she was taught the Word. She acted as a woman of integrity, virtue, and influence. Therefore, she could identify that situation with the Word of God. "Forgive those who have wrongfully used you. The weak must bear the infirmity of the strong. "Brethren, if a man is overtaken, in a fault, ye who are spiritual restore such a one in the spirit of meekness, considering thyself, lest thou also be tempted. Bear ye one other's burdens, and so fulfill the Law of Christ".

"For if a man thinks himself to be something, when he is nothing, he deceived himself" (Gal. 6:1-3). Joyce Milton journalist, estimation while examining this formidable, fascinating woman, giving probing insight into the First lady's character, her values, and career.

Joyce Milton diligently searched out the First Lady's involvement in travel-gate, File gate, the Health Care Task Force fiasco, and fundraisings and for the 1996 presidential campaign showing how these controversies grew out of the tension in her political partnership with Bill Clinton. She went further to investigate Hillary Rodham's Midwest childhood and Methodist upbringing, when she developed a strong belief for religious faith. This Milton stated that "Hillary was the most admired woman in America while also becoming the most visibly wronged wife in the world".

Milton's continuous research of Hillary Rodham's Midwestern childhood and Methodist upbringing proved that she developed a strong belief that social and political activism can be woven together in one's religious faith. She was a student of Wellesley and a children's right advocate at Yale Law School. Where she became Bill Clinton's espoused wife. Her influence and knowledge were manifested with her first experience as a legal staff for the House Judiciary Committee. Hillary Rodham Clinton dared to run for President and successfully ran two elections.

This may be so according to society's opinion. However, Eve was the most beautiful thing God created, taken from Adam's side to be his helper. Adam was incomplete without Eve. "And the Lord God caused a deep sleep to fall upon Adam, and he slept, and he took one of his ribs and closed up the flesh instead thereof. And the rib, which the LORD God had taken from man and made him a woman, and brought her unto the man" (Gen 2 :21- 22). When he awoke from the operation table and open his eyes he saw Eve he said "That is now bone of my bones and flesh of my flesh I will call her woman" my good thing. "For he who finds a wife finds a good thing, and obtain favor from the LORD" (Pro. 18:22). A wife is God's gift to a man."

"And the LORD said, it is not good that the man should be alone; I will make him a helper fit for him (Gen. 2:18). "Woman the mother of all living."

The divine purpose relative to a woman is found in the first part of the first story of the Creation. So God created man in His own image, in the image of God, created He male and female, created He them (Gen. 1: 26 - 27; 2: 23). Here we have a warranty for woman's dominion, her power her influence.

The fact that God did not give man dominion until he had a woman his supportive system besides him is evidence of her exalted place in the Creation. The magnificent theme of the story is that the only true and wise God, The Omniscient God, The Faithful God who sees our hearts and supplies our needs, provided Adam with a helper to complete him "Eve" the giver of life.

All of the great qualities in a woman's life, her marriage, mating and motherhood, her career unfolds in all of her excellence in the Genesis account of Eve consist of her the family with all the joys and headaches came into being with Eve as the giver of life, her weakness to be deceived and sinned against God and her husband; her faith, influence, and valor to exercise her authority and to take dominion over the works of God's hand. "For in Adam all died, even so in Christ shall all be made alive, all have sinned and come short of the glory of God" (Rom.3:23).

"But God who is rich in mercy for His great love wherein He loves us, even when we were dead in sin, hath made us alive together with Christ "by grace you are saved" (Eph. 2: 5-8).

Being a virtuous and influential woman as Senator Clinton she dared to run as president in the 2008 election considering how increasingly difficult it would be to maintain her position as wife and mother and junior senator. However, she remained loyal to her country and stood up against the American presence in Iraq., Afghanistan, and Pakistan due to her experience being there, she rebuked President Bush for considering sending more troops to war.

Although she did not win the Presidential election, she proved her greatness in humility and work with singleness of heart with President Obama for the welfare of the American people and the blessedness of this enormous nation.

Nancy Pelosi, a wife a mother of five children while they were yet young she volunteered for Democratic candidates and causes. Her children raised and called her blessed; her husband also and praised her but as her children grew up, Pelosi continues her Democratic Party worked and became very instrumental in allocating funds for her Democratic Party. According to Elaine S. Povich, Pelosi who spent more than $1 million on her campaign, won election to the House, with 62 percent of the vote in the overwhelmingly Democratic district. Within a week later she was sworn into office.

Her bravery caused her to take up the banner of human rights in Chain, sponsoring a measure to allow Chinese students to remain in the United States after the Tiananmen Square massacre, and tries, without success, to end China's favored trade status. As a member of the Appropriations Committee, helps lead an effort to increase federal funding for programs to research ADL and provide services for those suffering from the disease.

In 1998 Petosi a kind and compass ate woman, as a member of the House Intelligence Committee, traveled to Guatemala to investigate the assassination of an activist Roman Catholic bishop, Juan Gerardo Conedera.

Nancy Pelosi was awarded the highest congressional whip party position among the minority. She was the first woman to be elected that position in 2001 and defeated her rival Rep. Her professionalism and perseverance granted her favor with the House of Democrats as their minority leader, making her the highest-ranking woman in the history of the house, Bush, after his successful-reelection, introduces a plan to change Social Security and created private investment accounts. Pelosi and the Democratic leadership fought the plan, holding their caucus together, and made Bush's plan so unpopular it never even reached the House floor. Democratic won 30 Republican House seats to take control of the body for the first time since 1994, Pelosi become the first woman Speaker of the House a woman of intelligence and influence.

The idea of Hillary Clinton's running for the presidency and Nancy Pelosi elevation to Speaker of the House has initiated the path that motivated American political women to exercise their potential.

It is said that" In the 230 years of this country's history, never has a woman let alone a mother and a grandmother risen to such a position of power as Nancy Pelosi did when she assumed her role as the first female Speaker of the House, third in line for the presidency". In his book "Madam Speaker" Marc Sandalow, an esteemed journalist and political analyst who covered Pelosi's for decades offer a richly nuanced portrait of the woman who made history. He charts Pelosi's political roots, honoring on her father, who spent five terms in Congressional Record under her bed. And goes on to examine how Pelosi, who didn't run for political office until she was 47 years old.

We can identify Nancy Pelosi with the woman of Proverb's 31. A woman of aspiration, of purpose, excellence, and resourceful who set goals and had proper perspective raising her family first and then fought for her position in Washington, and becoming the most influential voice in the history of America today. The woman of Proverbs chapter31 was the supporting system for her home and community. This woman is noted as a virtuous woman whose price exceeds rubies. She loves her husband and grooms him appropriately, she does him good his meals are ready when he comes home, he looks dignify when he is among his co-workers and colleagues; he does not need to look outside. She takes good care of her children in that they raised and called her blessed; her husband also and he praised her for being his help mate. She is a compassionate and caring woman who considers the poor and needed.

"Favour is deceitful, and beauty is vain but the woman who fears the LORD shall be praised. Give her of the fruit of her hands, and let her works praise her in the gates" (Pro. 31 :30-31).

The power of women's influence has reformed politics immensely in recent decades not only in America but globally. The author's Viewpoints encourages women to become more involved in the US and World politics. However, we have women who have developed enough courage to do so. "Madam Speaker" Marc Sandalow, and esteemed journalist and political analyst who covered Pelosi's for decades offer a richly nuanced portrait of the woman who made history. He charts Pelosi's political roots, honoring on her father, who spent five terms in Congressional Record under her bed. And goes on to examine how Pelosi, who didn't run for political office until she was 47 years old.

"Favour is deceitful, and beauty is vain but the woman who fears the LORD shall be praised. Give her of the fruit of her hands, and let her works praise her in the gates" (Pro-31:30-31).

The power of women's influence has reformed politics immensely in recent decades not only in America but globally. The author of Viewpoints encourages women to become more involved in the US and World politics. However, we have women who have developed enough courage to do so.

Connybeare and Howson, in their evaluation, suggested that the Corinthian church may have had 60,000 believers who were mostly women, newly converts from the pagan temples and the Jewish synagogues.

Those women who were just liberated in Christ Jesus enjoyed their new freedom since there were no spiritual distinctions between male and female believers (Gal. 3:28).

"W.H. Ramsay. who researched and wrote said, "In Asia Minor, women had equality with men. During this period Roman women were elevated to full and equal status without any distinction between the sexes.

Chapter 7

JOAN OF ARC

"IT IS NOTED BY SUSAN Banfield in her book, "World Leaders Past and Present," Joan of Arc's effort to make King Charles a victorious warrior was accomplished after her death. Her special power and influence did not stop with those who knew her, despite the inevitable tragic outcome of her life, her story is still affecting people today. Although in her time, Joan never received permission to decorate her royal banner with the Fleur Delis. King Charles granted her family the name "Delys". Joan of Arc will always be remembered as a fighter at the siege of Orleans.

Joan mounted the pole with a pile of wood and sticks at the base of the scaffold nailing her to the pole, Joan's only request was for someone to go to the church, and get her crucifix which she bonded to a long stick holding it close by her face so that she might have the comfort of gazing on it once during her last moments.

The flames rose very fast and lasted for several minutes but all that was heard was the piercing cries of a young girl; "Jesus, Jesus, Jesus" and it was all over. After her death her real character was unleashed in the world and the loyalty to her faith which brought inspiration to the men giving them courage to complete the great accomplishment, in liberating Orleans and crowning King Charles.

The measure of her integrity remained unshaken even unto death her extraordinary inspiration and influence became greater than ever before to the world. The news of Joan's tragic end awakened and deepened the loyalty of the people of France to their King and country, they were motivated to scatter the foreigners from their land which they could not do previously for the English had triumphed over France for many decades. Even the English were in deep remorse for burning a saint, most of all were King Charles, who did not give her the support she needed from him during her lifetime. Because of his crafty enemies, King Charles was intimidated by Joan's influence and equality. Nevertheless, Joan burning at the stake made him into the type of King Joan believed he could be even to the point that he was given the nickname Charles the Victorious by historians.

Memories were a part of his life which brought the transformation in as, much as trying to atone for the ungratefulness of his youth to the one who caused him to own a crown and a kingdom. He made several attempts to clear Joan's name of heresy but was unsuccessful although it went on for years yet Charles persisted.

Chapter 8

THE GREAT CONTROVERSY

WOMEN WHO CHANGED THE COURSE OF HISTORY IN THE NEW TESTAMENT.

THIS CHAPTER IS DELIBERATELY REPEATED to define the meaning of"Let A Woman Be Silent In Church". (1Cor.14:33-34). The apostle Paul was addressing the customs of the Jews in those days. The customarily settings in the Synagogues were that men sat on one side and women on the other; even at the wailing wall in Jerusalem today the custom is practiced. However, some of the finest leaders in Israel were women. Considering that, culture was male dominated while women were subservience.

Research, and diligent study has proven that the "Gospel was a liberating Force in Ancient World"; challenging and reforming old and established doctrine that were imbedded in human prejudice were reformed, thanks be to God. " But, you Daniel shut up the words, and seal the book until the time of the end; many shall run to and fro, and knowledge shall increase" (Dan. 12:4). Discrimination and lack of knowledge of who women were, caused Rabbinic teachings to be hostile towards women. Considered, Jewish tradition, Rabbis were admonished not to teach or even speak to women. They seem inefficient to be part of the count needed when a Synagogue had to be established.

When Paul stated that women should keep silent in the church he was addressing order in the house of God, while they were sublimate under the law, that women should be submissive as the "Law says" (1 Cor. 14:33-34). But Jesus is the end of the Law to all Righteousness. He liberated women. "And you shall know the truth, and the Truth, shall make you free"(John 8:32).

However, Luke shaded the light in his writing that both men and women were in the Upper Room on the Day of Pentecost, and they were all filled with the Holy Ghost (Acts 2:4). They were all persecuted and were instrumental in the growth of the early church. Reference scriptures (Acts 5:14; 8:12; 9:2; 17:4;).

THE LOVE OF GOD KNOWS NO GENDER BOUNDARIES.

Jesus makes the difference. Women who enjoy all the fullness of the Holy Spirit embraced God's purpose for their lives and accepted the challenge of ancient tradition which began with Jesus early ministry and were devoted servants for the Lord.

Many women were generous partners with Jesus' ministry and to his disciples. They were hospitable to him. Reference scriptures. (Matt. 27: 55 - 56; Luke 10: 40 - 41; Luke 8:3). In virtue of the fact that Mary sat at the feet of Jesus; She was favored with the honor that was most likely given to men according to the Gospel. Women were also honored to proclaim the exciting event which the disciples were long awaiting "The Resurrection of Jesus Christ".

Mary Magdalene was the first to see "Jesus, the risen LORD" and was commissioned by Him, "Go! and tell My Disciples." (THIS

FIRST WOMAN EVANGELIST.) Mary Magdalene was the last one to leave the tomb while the men were gone. And the first one who came back early in the morning.

In the inception of the Apostolic Church women were instrumental in the ministry such as Dorcas or Tabitha who was called a "disciple"(Acts 9:36). Peter was summoned to leave where he was and to come to pray for Dorcas to be restored to life, for the community could not survived without her.

Another woman who was very generous in supporting the ministry was John Mark's mother; who used her house as the worship center for the Jerusalem church. The believers found peace and security as they broke bread, prayed and had all things in command. While Herod Agrippa was persecuting the church. How can we forget Lydia? a philanthropy who used her resources to enhance the Women's Ministry. She was not like that rich ruler who was sorrowful and walked away from Jesus when Jesus asked him to give what he had to the poor because he had much wealth. But Lydia valued her salvation, because she realized that her wealth could not redeem her.

Therefore, she honored the men of God who took time to show her the way to God. She invited them to her home (Acts16:14-15). The women of the early church were instrumental in the ministry, they were powerful and influential in their praying, teaching, giving and propagating the gospel of Jesus Christ. These were women of Faith, Pioneers of whom Women Ministry became a key component of the work of the Church.

When the Apostle Paul commended Titus and Timothy as "fellow workers" with him, he also classified Andronicus and Junias who seemed to be husband and wife as outstanding among the Apostles (Rom.16:7).

A woman of power, a woman of influence in the New Testament was Priscilla her husband was Aquila, who was newly converted and were deported from Rome. She and her husband embraced Paul and worked with him in the craft of tent making, recognizing him as a "Man of God"(Acts 18:1-3). They were passionate in the growth of the church in Rome and by so doing somehow risking their lives for the cause of the gospel (Rom.16:3-5) Priscilla and her husband showed brotherly kindness to Apollos, the eloquent preacher from Alexandria and tutored him diligently in the Word of the Lord.

How could such a woman like Pricilla who could rightly divide the "Word of Truth" remain silent? Her influence, and courage caused their ministry to be known and widespread. And by virtue of their fame was evidenced for Apostle Paul to give reference to them in his writing. Reference scriptures (Rom.16:3; 1 Cor. 16:19; 2 Tim. 4:19)

NEW TESTAMENT HEROINS OF FAITH:

(1) Phoebe (Rom.16:1-2). She was that type of a woman of great courage and perseverance who took Apostle Paul's letter to the Romans. Phoebe was recommended to the Lord by the Apostle Paul to the Roman Church requesting that she was recognized as the Saints. And was worthy of any assistance they could offer her. Paul also commended her as an efficient worker in the ministry.

Phoebe's influence and faith qualified her to be a woman equal with men in the ministry, and that the Roman Church should support her according to Paul's request (Rom.16:1-2).

Philip the evangelist had four daughters who functioned in the early church as prophetess (Acts 21:9). Paul's instruction to women praying or prophesying in a worship environment did not exempt Philip's daughters (1 Cor. 11:5). Women of destiny who were filled with the Holy Spirit were desirous to be used of God whatever the nature of the ministry was and were used by God and devoted themselves to the will of God and functioned efficiently for the work of God.

Women contributed to a fundamental role in the inception of Christianity. They did not compete with men but completed that of men by their leadership responsibilities. They were obedient and submissive which are as significant testimony of the liberating power of Jesus Christ.

Timing belongs to God. "But when the fullness of the time, had come; God sent forth His Son" born of a woman, born under the law, to redeem those who were under the law, that we might receive the adoption as sons"(Gal.4:4). God is the one who changes the times and the seasons. (Dan. 2:21). He removes kings and rises up kings, He gives wisdom to the wise. And knowledge to those who have Understanding "He has given women the authority to use their influence to exemplify Christ and change the course of their world.

After the death of the apostles the mantle of leadership passed on to a new generation which women gravitated to and are doing great exploits for the kingdom of God using the authority and their influence; Since there is neither Jew nor Greek, there is neither slave nor free, "there is neither male nor female; for we are all one in Christ Jesus" (Gal. 3:28).

CONCLUSION

"IN HER BOOK, HELENE AsHKER said that women were desirous to be completed during the 1980s since they were surrounded by the high society of technology. Women are turning their energy to be used like that of men, to excel, and succeed equally in the ministry. Many women have challenged men's area of activity and have met in some cases, even surpassed their goals. Women have excelled in top leadership positions, in the corporate boardroom, the military, the sports arena, mid academia. Women held cabinet offices in the government, and have won seats in the House of Congress and even chair on the Supreme Court. In the spiritual arena, women are binding together to continue their desire to fill the void to explore Christianity and to flourish, which only Christ can fill as opportunities are given to them to exercise their leadership abilities. Peter's wife was dormant while Peter was at home, but when Jesus called Peter to follow Him the privilege was hers to prove her leadership ability as she ministered and was hospitable to the crowd. How could she remain silent when the need demanded the power which was in her to be exercised?

The Author's goal in writing this book is to help women not to usurp authority over the men but to equip women with the scriptures to hurdle the obstacles of fear and criticism that may be preventing them from using their leadership abilities.

Women should equip themselves with knowledge through the use of history books to assist them in taking up leadership roles as given to them in the Bible. Every opportunity must be seized in order to be Leaders Of Today because Jesus has liberated women and given them the power and the authority to be effective leaders in the ministry.

De Gaulle was one of the greatest French military and political figures during that century who had a special devotion to Joan and while reading the story of her death his life also ended. Joan brought such awakening to the French nationalists and Catholics that they were inspired to live up to their convictions. The passing of time did not deter her power and attraction whereby canonizing her as a saint by the Roman Catholic Church. Even young girls in need of courage and honesty turn to Joan's story daily. There are yet thousands, from the least to the greatest who is being admonished by Joan's leadership, courage, loyalty, and heroism. She is portrayed surrounded by the saints who communicated to her burning proving that death did not separate her from what she held dear to her heart but was faithful to her voices promoting her legend to the end. "Let your manner of life be without covetousness, and be content with such things as we have, for he hath said, He will never leave thee, nor forsake thee. So that we may boldly say, the Lord is my helper, and I will not fear what man shall do unto me." Hebrews 13: 5-6 KJV by the help of God, Joan of Arc truly demonstrated her abilities as a leader equal to men in the ministry."

MARCELLA

"IT IS SAID OF EDITH Deen that Marcella could be an effective leader equal to men in the ministry in her book "Great Women of the Christian Faith", Marcella wealthy and beautiful woman of Rome. Her love of the scriptures and her leadership of the fourth-century community of Christian women, her most lasting fame is as the founder of the first convent in the Western Church. Marcellus received inspiration for this as a little girl, when Marcella's mother Albina extended hospitality to Athanasius, Patriarch of Alexandria, who was then in exile. She listened spellbound while this venerable prelate told of the monks living in the Egyptians desert. The memory of the monk's example never left and maleness is to be celebrated as one of God's gifts." So Therefore we should give Him glory. There should be no classification of the fruit of the spirit because God makes no distinction. The Christian character is produced by the Holy Spirit, not by self-effort according to (John 15:1-5) and (Galatians 5:22).

Acknowledgement

I AM PLEASED TO TAKE this opportunity to thank my colleagues, friends and faculty members who have helped me with this research project. I am most indebted to my God who has given me the courage to persevere to aspire me to share my influence by writing this book. I would also like to thank my husband Pastor Julian Polidore. Finally, I thank all my prayer partners for interceding on my behalf when I was too exhausted to pray. I give God all the glory for the gift and knowledge to write. I dedicated this book to my four daughters to admonish and inspire them to emulate my faith and use their influence whenever the opportunity presents itself.

Dr. Joan A. Polidore

www.ingramcontent.com/pod-product-compliance
Lightning Source LLC
Chambersburg PA
CBHW041629140626
46547CB00031B/1816